Free.

WELC

MW00425512

YOUR NAME HERE:

*3:17

2 CORINTHIANS

WHERE THE SPIRIT OF THE LORD IS,
THERE IS FREEDOM.

© 2010 by Brian Tome

All rights reserved. No portion of this book
may be reproduced, stored in a retrieval
system, or transmitted in any form or
by any means—electronic, mechanical,
photocopy, recording, scanning, or
other—except for brief quotations in critical
reviews or articles, without the prior written
permission of the publisher.

Published in Nashville, Tennessee,
by Thomas Nelson. Thomas Nelson is a
trademark of Thomas Nelson, Inc.

Thomas Nelson, Inc., titles may be
purchased in bulk for educational,
business, fund-raising, or sales promotional
use. For information, please e-mail
SpecialMarkets@ThomasNelson.com.

All Scripture quotations, unless otherwise
indicated, are taken from the HOLY BIBLE:
NEW INTERNATIONAL VERSION®.
© 1973, 1978, 1984 by International Bible
Society. Used by permission of Zondervan
Publishing House. All rights reserved.

**Library of Congress Cataloging-
in-Publication Data on file with the
Library of Congress.**

ISBN: 978-0-8499-4655-4

Printed in the United States of America

09 10 11 12 13 14 RRD 9 8 7 6 5 4 3 2 1

THANKFULLY, GETTING FREE REQUIRES MORE THAN SELF-HELP.

While you'll learn new things and need to roll up your sleeves as you interact with this guide, ultimate freedom comes through a relationship with Jesus and is far greater than the sum of your efforts.

TRUE FREEDOM IS A GIFT FROM GOD.

For some simple tips on interacting with this guide, check out page 98.

"Freeeeeeeeeeeeeeeeeeeeeeeeeeeeeeeeeeeeeeeeeeeeeeeeeeeeeeeeeeeeeeeeeeeeeeeeeeeeeeeeeeeeeeeeeeeee

THIS ISN'T YOUR TYPICAL WORKBOOK.

This is an interactive guide to discovering at least one thing that's holding you back from the free, full life God intends for you.*

What you choose to do about that thing is up to you. But know this: God really wants you to be free, and he's got more than enough power to make it happen. He wants you to experience the kind of freedom and joy you thought only kids could have. But beginning this journey is up to you.

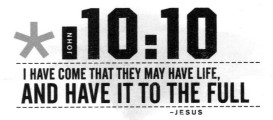

*JOHN 10:10
I HAVE COME THAT THEY MAY HAVE LIFE,
AND HAVE IT TO THE FULL
-JESUS

ONE

WELCOME TO YOUR FREEDOM STORY

Do you ever act out of guilt?

Do you ever worry what others will think?

Are you bored a lot?

Being free means more than choosing your career, living in America, or voting for the politician of your choice. It involves more than simply making your own decisions, staying out of jail, or even being "saved."

TOTAL FREEDOM MEANS LIVING COMPLETELY FEARLESSLY, PASSIONATELY AND JOYFULLY— REGARDLESS OF YOUR CIRCUMSTANCES, NOT BECAUSE OF THEM.

Are you free?

The Bible says,

"Where the spirit of the Lord is, there is freedom." ✶

Not fear.
Not guilt.
Not morality or religion.

Freedom.

Maybe you've never thought of it this way, but at its heart, the Bible is a freedom story. It begins with God giving Adam and Eve free will in the Garden of Eden, and it follows the plight of the nation of Israel— from their struggle to escape the bondage of slavery in Egypt through their deliverance into the freedom of God's Promised Land.

But this grand freedom story is so much bigger than one nation's escape from slavery. Just as God delivered the Israelites from bondage thousands of years ago, he's still in the business of setting people free.

Throughout this guide, you'll see real-life examples of how other people experience God's freedom—from where they started to where they are now. Because sometimes we need to hear that other people share similar backgrounds and hang-ups. And we need to hear what's on the other side.

✶ **STORY**

RACHEL
DORA
DAVID
BRETT
SCOTT
MICHAEL
KRISSY
COURTNEY

You, too, are part of a freedom story that's unfolding. God is the author, and you have a vital role to play.

2 CORINTHIANS ✶**3:17**

Some of the areas of our lives where we think we're the most free can actually be the places where we're unknowingly held hostage.

THE NEXT SEVERAL PAGES INCLUDE A SELF-ASSESSMENT TO HELP IDENTIFY SOME PLACES WHERE WE MIGHT BE EXPERIENCING SOMETHING LESS THAN TRUE FREEDOM.

Be as honest as you can. This process is for you.

WHAT'S A DREAM YOU HAVE RIGHT NOW THAT YOU'RE NOT PURSUING?

It could be related to your job, your relationships, your passion, your spirituality.
Write about it, make a list, or sketch it out.

"I'm sick of following my dreams.
I'm just going to ask them where they're going and hook up with them later."
—MITCH HEDBERG

WHY AREN'T YOU PURSUING THAT DREAM?

List the reasons—good or bad, practical, or otherwise—that hold you back.

★ STORY

RACHEL

I over-thought every decision to the point of exhaustion.

full story on page 100

MICHAEL

I was afraid of making a mistake.

full story on page 104

COURTNEY

I morphed into what others wanted me to be.

full story on page 101

Free.*

Here are a bunch of phrases.

CIRCLE ANY THAT HIT CLOSE TO HOME.

Your gut will be the best guide, so this shouldn't take long. Of course, they're not all pretty, and your inner critic might shout, **"No! Don't circle *that* one!"** But if you're honest, "that one" definitely gets the pen lasso. So go ahead. Circle whatever feels like part of your life.

- ■ I have a hard time being corrected.

- ■ My family comes first, no matter what.

- ■ I don't want to draw attention to myself.

- ■ I feel better about myself when other people reveal their problems.

- ■ I compare my spiritual life to what others do or don't do.

- ■ I hate being seen as emotional.

- ■ God is disappointed with me.

- ■ Sometimes I lie to keep the peace.

- ■ My prayer time feels like a burden.

- ■ I bleed my team's (or country's) colors.

- ■ I don't take criticism well.

- ■ It's hard when people don't notice the good things I do.

- If I had more money, I'd be more generous.

- I want people to know that I go to church.

- I often feel left out, or worry that I will be.

- I'm worried I might lose my salvation.

- I'm proud of my strong morals.

- I judge others more often than I like to admit.

- I can do it best.

- I want others to know about the pain in my past.

- I have too much baggage.

- No one understands me.

- I blame the church.

- I want people to notice my pain or what I'm up against.

- I don't want to appear weak.

- I don't speak up.

- I want people to notice the way I stand out.

- I'm a perfectionist.

- No one will take care of me.

- Nobody tells me what to do.

- I don't really believe God will (or can) provide.

- I need to outperform the people I work with.

- I've thought about suicide.

- I can't forgive myself.

- I'm worried I'll say something stupid.

- I can't imagine living without alcohol.

- Difficult conversations and confrontations are hard for me.

- I have a hard time trusting authority.

- There is at least one person I can't forgive.

- I like people to know I'm busy—always in meetings, always on the go.

- I take offense to things easily.

- God has allowed some things to happen to me that aren't fair.

- I'm angry more often than I'd like to be.

- Economic downturns keep me up at night.

- I can unleash a verbal beat-down with the best of them.

- I think some people should just burn in hell.

- I'm worried I might run out of money.

- I crave attention.

- I feel abandoned.

- I'm depressed.

- I have secrets I can't tell.

- I like to escape.

- I like being considered "mysterious."

- I need to feel like the smartest person in the room.

- I feel nervous a lot.

- I'm afraid I don't measure up.

- I feel like I don't belong.

- I'm upset about my past a lot.

Free.*

HAS BEEN SAID OF YOU

FIRST

Check any of the following phrases that you recall being said to you or about you (whether you think it was a fair judgement or not).

SECOND

Next to anything that you checked, write what you think that comment might indicate about a way you behave or something you might believe.

(For instance, if you checked *"I have to walk on eggshells around you,"* you might write, *"I can be overly-sensitive"* or *"I like to be in control."*)

☐ You really should ask for help.

☐ You're all talk.

☐ I'd hate to be on your bad side.

☐ You always have to be right.

☐ I just don't feel like I can trust you.

☐ I have to walk on eggshells around you.

☐ You take things too seriously.

☐ Sometimes you don't let people in.

☐ I just can't figure you out.

☐ You shouldn't worry so much.

☐ People aren't out to get you.

☐ You have good ideas, they just don't seem to get done.

☐ You just don't seem happy.

☐ You should slow down.

☐ Can you be serious?

☐ Maybe it's time you tried it on your own.

☐ It seems like you always need to be in a relationship.

☐ Didn't you already forgive her/him?

☐ It's hard to have a real conversation with you.

☐ You're such a perfectionist.

☐ You just need to let it go.

WHY?

God loves and accepts you. He offers you forgiveness and wants to be in relationship with you.

(Sometimes accepting and really believing this is hard.)

Our perceptions of God and how he views us get skewed by all kinds of experiences: imperfect parents, church baggage, bad relationships, you name it. As a result, most of us walk around with wrong ideas about who God is and how he desires to relate to us.

Identifying those false beliefs is the first step to breaking free from them.

CIRCLE ANYTHING THAT SEEMS LIKE A WAY YOU SOMETIMES VIEW GOD, OR THINK HE VIEWS YOU.

(Be as honest as you can—God's not threatened by any of this.)

I feel guilty
asking God for
some things.

I'm scared
of God.

God has a lot
on his plate—I'm not
that important.

God really
can't (or won't)
forgive me.

God loves
other people more
than me.

I think God
owes me certain
things.

God is just
waiting for me to
screw up.

God is
disappointed
in me.

I need to clean
up my act before
God will love me.

God isn't
listening.

Sometimes
I'm not sure if I'm
really "saved."

I need to
provide for myself—
God won't do that.

I should
work harder to
serve God.

There are
some things God
won't forgive.

Getting closer
to God kind of
freaks me out.

My relationship
with God is up to
me to control.

Free.*

CHOOSE THREE

Flip through your responses over the last few pages, and write down the three statements that stand out to you the most—whether something you wrote, circled or checked.
Write them here:

1

2

3

NOW, CHOOSE JUST ONE

Select the statement that resonates with you the most. It might be something you've always known was a hang-up or maybe it's something you hadn't considered but realize has a strong foothold in your life. Now might be a great opportunity to take a moment to invite God to point you in the direction he wants you to go.

Once you've picked one, write it in the space provided and proceed.

1

(Questions about prayer? Turn to page 99.)

18

There's a reason you picked that statement. It's probably related to something you believe about yourself, or about God.

If that belief isn't immediately apparent to you, simply evaluate the statement you wrote down at face value and ask yourself, **"why?"** You'll probably need to ask and answer "why" a few times until the underlying belief becomes clear.

KRISSY'S EXAMPLE
STATEMENT:
I can do it best.

WHY? I have great attention to detail.

WHY? I'm really a perfectionist.

WHY? I'd hate to mess up or drop the ball.

WHY? I can't lose the recognition of being someone who doesn't fail.

THIS MAKES ME REALIZE I MIGHT BELIEVE:

My identity and worth is tied to what I accomplish.

WHY? _____

WHY? _____

WHY? _____

WHY? _____

THIS MAKES ME REALIZE I MIGHT BELIEVE:

Free.*

GALATIANS 5:1

✶ IT IS FOR FREEDOM THAT CHRIST HAS SET US FREE. STAND FIRM, THEN, AND DO NOT LET YOURSELVES BE BURDENED AGAIN BY A YOKE OF SLAVERY.

If we want more freedom in our lives—even in ways that seem small—we need to take an honest look at the day-to-day things we do and the things we've come to believe about ourselves, about other people, and about God.

Usually, it's not obvious how we're getting trapped. On the surface, the beliefs and behaviors that hold us back might even seem like good things, or like ways we protect ourselves ("I can take care of myself"). But those beliefs often have an ugly flipside rooted in fear ("I never let anyone help me because I know they'll let me down").

But here's some incredible news: Jesus came to set us free.✶

■ ■■■

Whether we realize it or not, it's God at the center of our stories—not pain, not bad situations, not problems or bad habits. So just in case you're tempted right now to crawl off to a corner and start dwelling on your hang-ups, resist that temptation. Stand firm.

God's offering freedom, and that's where we're headed.

PRAY

Spend a few minutes asking God to help you identify the unhealthy beliefs and behaviors in your life that stand in the way of your freedom. Ask Him if there's anything specific he wants you to see. Then ask Him to show you what freedom means.

LUKE

4:18-19 *

"The Spirit of the Lord is on me, because he has anointed me to proclaim good news to the poor. He has sent me to proclaim freedom for the prisoners and recovery of sight for the blind, to set the oppressed free, to proclaim the year of the Lord's favor."
–Jesus

TWO

You were running a good race. Who cut in on you to keep you from obeying the truth? That kind of persuasion does not come from the one who calls you. "A little yeast works through the whole batch of dough." GALATIANS **5:7-9**

Just as the smallest amount of yeast works though an entire batch of dough, believing even the smallest lie about ourselves or God has all kinds of effects, often in many areas of our lives. And wherever we're sidetracked by a lie, we're in bondage to it. We're not free.

So, let's explore that belief you identified in the last section a little further. Let's discover some of the ways it's infiltrated your life, and its effects. Then we'll hold it up to what God has to say about you in the Bible. Because the God who created you knows the truth about you.

And the truth will set you free.[*]

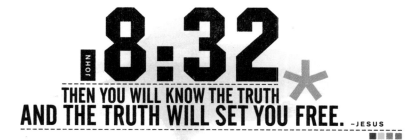

JOHN **8:32** ✳
THEN YOU WILL KNOW THE TRUTH
AND THE TRUTH WILL SET YOU FREE. –JESUS

WRITE DOWN THE BELIEF YOU IDENTIFIED.
THEN EXPLORE.

Statement from page 19

Can you tie this
back to anything?

How has this belief
seemed to benefit you?

When does this feel like freedom?

What does this say about
a way you've grown up?

How has this affected the way
you act at home, work, or school?

When do you most notice the
ways this belief plays out?

Who does this belief affect
the most, other than you?

Free.*

Look back to your last exploration.

WHAT CONNECTIONS OR PATTERNS DO YOU NOTICE ABOUT THE WAY THIS BELIEF HAS PLAYED OUT IN YOUR LIFE?

STORY *

SCOTT

KRISSY

DAVID

RACHEL

I thought what I did defined who I was.
full story on page 102

I thought New Age spirituality would enlighten me.
full story on page 106

I worried that God's love was conditional.
full story on page 105

I used to agonize over my own sin.
full story on page 100

Having considered this belief from a few different angles,

HOW DOES IT MAKE YOU FEEL?

(Feelings can be good indicators of something going on beneath the surface.)

BRETT

My identity was completely tied to my alma mater.

full story on page 107

DORA

I felt rejected by everyone.

full story on page 103

COURTNEY

I believed God loved other people more than me.

full story on page 101

MICHAEL

I lived in fear of rocking the boat.

full story on page 104

Free.*

27

Untrue beliefs we've accepted as truth—consciously or unconsciously—can become "strongholds" in our lives that keep us in bondage. And until we recognize and choose to deal with them, they stand.

The good news? God has the power to bust-up any stronghold that's been established in your life, no matter how deeply it's entrenched or how long it's been fortified. And if you've chosen to follow Jesus, he's given you the authority to do the same.

While there are many types of strongholds, for the most part, the lies that hold us hostage fall into one of four main categories.

Turn back to the first section of this guide, and tally the total number of statements you circled or marked in each color.

TALLY

■ **RED STATEMENTS:**

■ **YELLOW STATEMENTS:**

■ **GREEN STATEMENTS:**

■ **BLUE STATEMENTS:**

COLORBLIND?
USE THIS KEY:
■ = RED
■ = YELLOW
■ = GREEN
■ = BLUE

WHICH COLOR HAS THE HIGHEST TOTAL?

If your totals are fairly even or there's not one clear "winner," that's OK. In that case, choose the color of the single, main statement you identified on page 18.

Either way, don't agonize over this. There's good stuff in all directions. You can always go through this process again, and you can explore as many paths as you want.

FOR RED, TURN TO PAGE: **30**

FOR YELLOW, TURN TO PAGE: **32**

FOR GREEN, TURN TO PAGE: **34**

FOR BLUE, TURN TO PAGE: **36**

Free.*

Red statements are mostly associated with the stronghold of Bitterness.

BITTER. ANGRY.

When you've made the decision—whether consciously or unconsciously—to hold onto hurts or perceived violations of your rights by refusing to forgive, you're choosing bitterness. When you insist on holding onto that grudge, you're doing so at the cost of your own freedom.

You might be bitter or angry about almost anything: individuals, the government, groups of people with different beliefs, or even that sports team you love to hate. Regardless of its focus, bitterness always leads you into a legalistic view of the world and away from the message of grace, because it concentrates your attention on the ways you feel you've been wronged.

And the result? Bitterness cuts you off from others.

While grace leads to unity and reconciliation (and freedom), bitterness and anger lead to isolation. Because when you're bitter, you separate yourself from whoever has wronged you. And so you're left alone to wallow in your judgment of others, or worse.

Bitterness—a failure to forgive— can even cause you to want some type of revenge, leading to anger, hatred, violence, and even murder. (While that sounds extreme, "murder" with our minds or mouths happens more often that we'd like to admit.)

Everyone has opportunities for bitterness because we've all been wronged. We've all been rejected or hurt at some point. But the way you choose to react when that happens leads to either freedom or bondage.

BITTERNESS AND ANGER DO NOT BRING FREEDOM.

STORY

★ To read two people's stories about overcoming Bitterness, turn to pages 100–101.

FORGIVEN.
GRACEFUL.

To be free of bitterness, you must receive and give forgiveness.

Jesus said that the person who's been forgiven the most, loves the most. That means that when you recognize judgment or unforgiveness in your own heart, you've got to go to God and receive more forgiveness for yourself. Because when you realize how much you've been forgiven, love and grace for others spring forth.

When you've walked away from bitterness, you feel free. You don't get your feelings hurt easily, and you're slow to condemn or even criticize others. You give people the benefit of the doubt, and you shy away from absolutes like, "she NEVER responds well to correction" or "he ALWAYS misunderstands." You're graceful.

And when you're free from bitterness, people want to be around you. Your friendships include people who've wronged you and have been reconciled to you again and again. You don't expect to find perfect friends—you take people as they are, bearing with whatever weaknesses they may have. People realize they don't have to be perfect to enjoy your acceptance.

When you are free from bitterness, you're happy to show mercy and offer forgiveness. You're experiencing how giving away grace cements your own freedom.

THIS BRINGS FREEDOM.

MATTHEW 6:14
LUKE 6:37
JOHN 15:12-13
EPHESIANS 4:32-5:2
COLOSSIANS 3:13
JAMES 2:12-13
1 JOHN 1:9

TURN TO PAGE 38

Free.*

Yellow statements are mostly associated with the stronghold of Rejection.

REJECTED.UNLOVED.

When you believe in the lie that you're rejected and unlovable, you are always on guard. You expect rejection. You anticipate bad endings.

You either push others away to prevent further rejection, or you desperately seek the approval, affirmation, and love of others. Your identity comes from what other people say about you and to you (not from the truth spoken by God). Sometimes this desperation to get others' approval can make you cling to any true friend who comes along. You take more from the relationship than you give; you're often needy and in a state of crisis.

On the other hand, if you react to feeling rejected and unloved by pushing others away, you're seen as cold or unemotional. You become suspicious of people's motives because you expect to be hurt, betrayed, or let down. But this is a defense: it feels safer not to fully express yourself. Sometimes, you even convince yourself that you don't require the kind of love that others require.

Self-hatred is one of the calling cards of rejection. You might disguise self-hatred with things like a larger-than-life personality, aggressive charisma or flashy possessions. But that front hides a fear of failing and being cast aside as "common" or not worth love. Self-hatred and doubt can lead you to dismiss the love offered in

Jesus. It also can drive you to over-performance and perfectionism. ("If people can't love me for me, I'll earn their love at all costs.") This mindset creates imbalance and unhealthy habits like body worship, workaholism, chemical addiction, sexual promiscuity, or depression.

Rejection can also make you act out in socially unacceptable ways. You might put yourself in situations where you'll almost definitely be rejected—an "I told you so"... to yourself. Rejected people scrutinize the actions of others and can replay conversations and situations with staggering accuracy, although the meaning and intent becomes twisted. You focus on your rejection and relate everything to it. ("Why did I say this at the party? I'm sure everyone noticed...they're probably still talking about it.")

When you believe the lie of being rejected, you get caught in a spiral of need, isolation, and self-doubt.

THIS IS NOT FREEDOM.

STORY

* To read two people's stories about overcoming Rejection, turn to pages 102–103.

ACCEPTED.LOVED.

When you are free from the lie of rejection, you are completely secure in the identity given to you by God. You don't crave or rely on the praise or approval of others because you believe you are deeply loved and accepted by God.

God's acceptance of you rates above other's opinions. You know you are accepted. You know you are loved.

Being free from rejection means you're free to serve others. You can deal with people without expectation because you're satisfied in God. You don't walk around with a hole in your heart, assuming people will continue to widen it. You can graciously receive love and support.

Self-hatred is not in you. God's opinion of you is the definitive statement on the matter—not your own opinion or other's. You receive that you are God's child, and with a humble spirit you know that you are an important, gifted, and loved member of his family. You are worthy, perfect in spirit, pure, holy, loved. You believe God did not make a mistake when creating you.

You believe you are wonderfully made. Your self-concept is stable and appropriate—not thinking of yourself too highly, but neither do you insult yourself out of a false humility.

You love from a place of overflow, not need. You give because you're grateful, not because you feel unworthy to be served. You can love others because you believe, deep in your heart, that you were loved first. By God.

THIS IS FREEDOM. THIS IS FOR YOU.

PSALM 139:13-14
ISAIAH 54:10
JOHN 1:12-13
GALATIANS 1:10
EPHESIANS 1:4-5
HEBREWS 2:11
HEBREWS 4:15
HEBREWS 10:22-23

TURN TO PAGE 38

Free.*

Green statements are mostly associated with the stronghold of Fear.

FEAR. STRESS.

When you are entrenched in fear, you're full of faith—but not the kind of faith that leads to life and freedom. Instead, your faith is in the expectation that bad things will happen. Stress (a.k.a. fear) overcomes you. Anxieties and worries are top of mind. And God's goodness and provision are a mirage.

Fear requires diligence, so you're constantly feeding it. You are your own protector; you have to navigate life's pitfalls; you have to provide for all your own needs. And you do this because you don't think anyone else (God included), can or will. You believe you are own best hope.

Fear is self-centered. ("God may have made all kinds of sweet-sounding promises, but I'm the exception, clearly. And those little verses may 'work' for some people, but not me. I'll take care of myself.") Pride supports fear like I-beams support a skyscraper.

Fear makes you feel alone, or like everything depends on you worrying your way out of trouble (which never happens). It says to God that he's either unable to deal with real needs, or just doesn't have the desire to meet those needs. Fear makes some awfully strong statements about God.

Being filled with fear means you have a hard time being open and transparent. You spend so much time and energy on your own protection or what-ifs that it seems counter-productive to share your hurts, needs, or frailty.

Your thoughts are consumed with worries about hopeless situations, threats, and possible disaster. Your hope in your fellow man is slight. You fall into the increasing confinement of your own ability.

FEAR IS A LIE.

STORY

★ To read two people's stories about overcoming Fear, turn to pages 104–105.

PEACE

Being free from fear means you believe God is greater than the world.

Instead of obsessing about the possible dangers in the future, you look forward to the promised provision of God. You believe God is sovereign—the complete answer—and that he is good. Regardless of current circumstances, being free of fear means you believe that God has the desire and ability to do what he promised: to protect and provide.

You believe God's heart is loving, like a Father toward his son, even when he allows pain or trouble. You know that our suffering is incomparable to the goodness that God engineers through it. You are not afraid of pain and you are not afraid of evil. You know God has won.

Because you're not out to protect yourself (because you trust God will do that), you don't hold tight to your life. You open up—and your life expands naturally, as a result. You love people who are hurting,

even when that love impinges on your "freedom". You give money to people with less, even though it de-insulates you for future needs. You don't attempt to live a predictable, controlled life. You are open to the unknown, to the mystery and wonder of God.

YOU LET GO OF THE WHAT-IFS.
YOU STAND CALM.
YOU LIVE BY FAITH.

THIS IS FREEDOM.

PSALM 23:4-6
PSALM 27:1
PSALM 27:13
HAGGAI 2:5
MATTHEW 6:25-34
JOHN 14:27
ROMANS 8:15
ROMANS 15:13
PHILIPPIANS 4:6-7
2 TIMOTHY 1:7
1 PETER 3:13-14
1 JOHN 4:18

TURN TO PAGE 38

Free.*

Blue statements are mostly associated with the stronghold of Religion.

RELIGION. PRIDE.

Religion holds you hostage. You are convinced that you have "earned it" or can earn it—if you just try harder. You measure your spiritual state by your activities, so your confidence in God's love relies on how many "bad" things you're avoiding and how much "good" you're doing: how much you are giving, how much you are volunteering, how many sacrifices you made today. Your good standing is a function of yourself, not of the finished work of Jesus.

You do not fling yourself upon the mercy and grace of God.

You focus on sin, both yours and others, and this strangles any joy and love. You follow rules line-by-line, and shut down the possibility that God speaks to people or that we can walk daily in God's Spirit. Your knowledge is encyclopedic; you might believe the Bible wholeheartedly, but not leave room for receiving it. You are often judgmental and self-righteous. Because you are aware and sensitive to "the rules" at all times, you expect others to be.

When you're religious, you operate on your own. No one is leading you or welcomed into a trusted role in your life. People know your name (and you often make sure they know you're part of a church and doing good things), but rarely do people know your hopes, gifts, or struggles. Instead of the confidence that comes from having the wisdom of a community around you, you are left to guess and work harder to make sense of life's dilemmas and mysteries.

You believe God needs you. You believe he is waiting for you to "make something of yourself," create a legacy, do some good in the world. You go back and forth between pride and insecurity. The more you advance into the ranks of your chosen religious expression, the more isolated you become, because all other people seem to be falling short.

Your mind is king. Your will is second in command. You don't need God.

THESE ARE LIES.

STORY

* To read two people's stories about overcoming Religion, turn to pages 106–107.

LOVE & GRACE

To be free means you are filled with grace. You receive and reflect the fullness of God's love.

Instead of working hard out of guilt or obligation, you believe God's condemnation or disappointment does not hang over you. You rest in the confidence of God's approval of you. You don't attempt to make God love you more, because you know this is impossible. And so your burden is light.

You trust Jesus. You believe you are covered by his protection and provision.

You believe your spirituality is based on relationships: you + God, you + others. You recognize that church is a network of relationships of believers of Jesus who submit to one another while they are in close relationship with him.

You believe God speaks to people and through people, and that he might redirect you and others at any point. You don't presume what God will say about anything. You put your faith in God, not in rules, laws, or organizations.

When you are free of religion, you don't judge others or try to measure their spirituality. You don't feel "better than" others. You are fully aware of your own forgiveness and that this did not come as an act of justice, but of mercy. You want others to experience that same mercy, favor, and kindness. Because of this, people see you as an encourager, a supporter, a person full of love. You overflow with grace.

YOUR LIFE IS SIMPLE. PURE. JOYFUL.

THIS IS WHAT IT MEANS TO BE FREE.

PSALM 23:1-3
MATTHEW 11:28-30
JOHN 1:12-13
JOHN 14:6
ACTS 17:24-25
ROMANS 4:4-5
ROMANS 8:1-2
EPHESIANS 2:8-9
HEBREWS 10:17-18
HEBREWS 12:2

TURN TO PAGE 38

Free.*

When we struggle with a stronghold, there's often a voice in our head that wants to dismiss anything that threatens the stronghold's power. So when we hear about things like God's acceptance, forgiveness, peace and love, we can be tempted to dismiss these as "wishful thinking."

But there's a difference between wishful thinking and thinking that's rooted in hope.

Hope looks forward to something that's founded in reality—something that's even more real than what we think or feel.*---

It's important to root our hope in what is true, especially when that truth feels uncomfortable or seems counter to what we're currently experiencing.

REAL FREEDOM IS BEING ABLE TO LIVE IN THE TRUTH IN SPITE OF OUR CIRCUMSTANCES. IT IS LIVING WITH AND STRUCTURING OUR LIVES AROUND HOPE.

That's where we're headed next.

HEBREWS **11:1**

*** NOW FAITH IS**
BEING SURE OF WHAT WE HOPE FOR
AND CERTAIN OF WHAT WE DO NOT SEE.

PRAY

Take a minute to ask God to help you see yourself as he sees you. Tell Him you want to experience life as he intends it: full, in freedom, and with hope.

THREE

The strongholds we've been exploring are the results of more than just petty fears, emotional baggage and bad memories. You shouldn't feel guilty about them. You shouldn't feel weak or beat yourself up over letting these beliefs creep into your life.

THE FACT IS: YOU'VE BEEN RIPPED OFF.

THIS FREEDOM STORY HAS A BAD GUY.

The Bible refers to dark characters in the spiritual realm as "demons" or "evil spirits," and they intend to steal life from us—to hold us hostage. The person in charge of these evil characters—the story's antagonist, our main adversary, the ultimate villain—is Satan.

The tricky thing is he usually doesn't manifest himself in our lives in a way that seems obvious, or scary. (Forget the horns, tail and pitchfork.) His approach is typically much more subtle, even seductive. Satan's trick is to twist the words of God into lies that seem reasonable or attractive in order to steal the freedom God intends for us.

But what was stolen from you has been recovered. Through Jesus, God has made the freedom he intended for you all along available again.

All you have to do is reclaim it.

READ THIS

Read this account of Jesus' interaction with Satan:

Then Jesus was led by the Spirit into the wilderness to be tempted by the devil. After fasting forty days and forty nights, he was hungry. The tempter came to him and said, "If you are the Son of God, tell these stones to become bread."

Jesus answered, "It is written: 'People do not live on bread alone, but on every word that comes from the mouth of God.'" * ---------------- *

DEUT. 8:3

Then the devil took him to the holy city and had him stand on the highest point of the temple. "If you are the Son of God," he said, "throw yourself down. For it is written: 'He will command his angels concerning you, and they will lift you up in their hands, so that you will not strike your foot against a stone.'"

Jesus answered him, "It is also written: 'Do not put the Lord your God to the test.'" *----------------- *

DEUT. 6:16

Again, the devil took him to a very high mountain and showed him all the kingdoms of the world and their splendor. "All this I will give you," *he said, "if you will bow down and worship me."*

Jesus said to him, "Away from me, Satan! For it is written: 'Worship the Lord your God, and serve him only.'" * --- *

DEUT. 6:13

Then the devil left him, and angels came and attended him. **MATTHEW**

4:1-11

Even Jesus was tempted by the devil. Notice how Satan twisted what Jesus knew to be true—even scripture—to try to get him to give in. Jesus could see that Satan was trying to manipulate him with a skewed version of the truth.

How did Jesus respond? By quoting scripture right back until the devil finally fled.

We've all bought into lies at some point along the way, and God wants to replace those lies with truth about who he is and who he created us to be.

Now, let's replace the lies we might have believed with truth from scripture. In the last section, if you were directed to the stronghold of:

BITTERNESS, TURN TO PAGE **44**■

REJECTION, TURN TO PAGE **46**

FEAR, TURN TO PAGE **48**■

RELIGION, TURN TO PAGE **50**■

Free.*

Are you easily angered or frustrated, or just can't seem to let things go? Do you tend to harbor resentment toward God or others? Have you never received forgiveness for yourself?

FORGIVENESS CAN SET YOU FREE.

Let's see what God has to say about the matter.

READ ALL OF THE FOLLOWING SCRIPTURES, AND CIRCLE ANY THAT REALLY SPEAK TO YOU.

■ MATTHEW **6:14**

For if you forgive men when they sin against you, your heavenly Father will also forgive you.

■ LUKE **6:37**

Do not judge, and you will not be judged. Do not condemn, and you will not be condemned. Forgive, and you will be forgiven.

■ JOHN **15:12–13**

My command is this: Love each other as I have loved you. Greater love has no one than this, that he lay down his life for his friends.

■ EPHESIANS **4:32–5:2**

Be kind and compassionate to one another, forgiving each other, just as in Christ God forgave you. Be imitators of God, therefore, as dearly loved children and live a life of love, just as Christ loved us and gave himself up for us as a fragrant offering and sacrifice to God.

■ COLOSSIANS **3:13**

Bear with each other and forgive whatever grievances you may have against one another. Forgive as the Lord forgave you.

■ JAMES **2:12–13**

Speak and act as those who are going to be judged by the law that gives freedom, because judgment without mercy will be shown to anyone who has not been merciful. Mercy triumphs over judgment!

■ 1 JOHN **1:9**

If we confess our sins, he is faithful and just and will forgive us our sins and purify us from all unrighteousness.

NOW, TURN TO PAGE 52

Free.*

Ever feel rejected by God or others, or like there's something you need to do to win their approval? Do you expect to be pushed away, or anticipate bad endings? Do you find yourself preoccupied with needing to be accepted?

ALL THAT CAN END RIGHT NOW.

Let's see what God has to say about the matter.

READ ALL OF THE FOLLOWING SCRIPTURES, AND CIRCLE ANY THAT REALLY SPEAK TO YOU.

PSALM 139:13–14
For you created my inmost being; you knit me together in my mother's womb. I praise you because I am fearfully and wonderfully made; your works are wonderful, I know that full well.

ISAIAH 54:10
"Though the mountains be shaken and the hills be removed, yet my unfailing love for you will not be shaken nor my covenant of peace be removed," says the LORD, who has compassion on you.

JOHN 1:12–13
Yet to all who received him, to those who believed in his name, he gave the right to become children of God—children born not of natural descent, nor of human decision or a husband's will, but born of God.

GALATIANS 1:10
Am I now trying to win the approval of men, or of God? Or am I trying to please men? If I were still trying to please men, I would not be a servant of Christ.

EPHESIANS 1:4–5
For [God] chose us in [Jesus] before the creation of the world to be holy and blameless in his sight. In love he predestined us to be adopted as his sons through Jesus Christ, in accordance with his pleasure and will…

HEBREWS 2:11
Both the one who makes men holy and those who are made holy are of the same family. So Jesus is not ashamed to call them brothers.

HEBREWS 4:15
For we do not have a high priest who is unable to sympathize with our weaknesses, but we have one who has been tempted in every way, just as we are—yet was without sin.

HEBREWS 10:22–23
Let us draw near to God with a sincere heart in full assurance of faith, having our hearts sprinkled to cleanse us from a guilty conscience and having our bodies washed with pure water. Let us hold unswervingly to the hope we profess, for he who promised is faithful.

NOW, TURN TO PAGE 52

Free.*

Are you stressed out a lot? Do anxiety and worry preoccupy your thoughts? Do you feel burdened by having to protect and provide for you and yours because you're sure no one else will?

BOO!! (Just kidding.)

Let's see what God has to say about the matter.

READ ALL OF THE FOLLOWING SCRIPTURES, AND CIRCLE ANY THAT REALLY SPEAK TO YOU.

PSALM 23:4-6
Even though I walk through the valley of the shadow of death, I will fear no evil, for you are with me; your rod and your staff, they comfort me. You prepare a table before me in the presence of my enemies. You anoint my head with oil; my cup overflows. Surely goodness and love will follow me all the days of my life, and I will dwell in the house of the LORD forever.

PSALM 27:1
The LORD is my light and my salvation— whom shall I fear? The LORD is the stronghold of my life— of whom shall I be afraid?

PSALM 27:13
I am still confident of this: I will see the goodness of the LORD in the land of the living.

HAGGAI 2:5
This is what I covenanted with you when you came out of Egypt. And my Spirit remains among you. Do not fear.

MATTHEW 6:25-27
Therefore I tell you, do not worry about your life, what you will eat or drink; or about your body, what you will wear. Is not life more important than food, and the body more important than clothes? Look at the birds of the air; they do not sow or reap or store away in barns, and yet your heavenly Father feeds them. Are you not much more valuable than they? Who of you by worrying can add a single hour to his life?

JOHN 14:27
Peace I leave with you; my peace I give you. I do not give to you as the world gives. Do not let your hearts be troubled and do not be afraid.

ROMANS 8:15
For you did not receive a spirit that makes you a slave again to fear, but you received the Spirit of sonship.

ROMANS 15:13
May the God of hope fill you with all joy and peace as you trust in him, so that you may overflow with hope by the power of the Holy Spirit.

PHILIPPIANS 4:6-7
Do not be anxious about anything, but in everything, by prayer and petition, with thanksgiving, present your requests to God. And the peace of God, which transcends all understanding, will guard your hearts and your minds in Christ Jesus.

2 TIMOTHY 1:7
For God has not given us a spirit of fear, but of power and of love and of a sound mind.

1 PETER 3:13-14
Who is going to harm you if you are eager to do good? But even if you should suffer for what is right, you are blessed. Do not fear what they fear; do not be frightened.

1 JOHN 4:18
There is no fear in love. But perfect love drives out fear, because fear has to do with punishment. The one who fears is not made perfect in love.

NOW, TURN TO PAGE 52

Free.*

Do you keep score? Ever thought you needed to clean yourself up before entering into a relationship with God? Ever believed that He'd love you more if you'd work a little harder, get better morals, or that your relationship with him was up to you to control?

THOSE ARE ALL LIES.

Let's see what God has to say about the matter.

READ ALL OF THE FOLLOWING SCRIPTURES, AND CIRCLE ANY THAT REALLY SPEAK TO YOU.

■ PSALM **23:1–3**
The LORD is my shepherd, I shall not be in want. He makes me lie down in green pastures, he leads me beside quiet waters, he restores my soul.

■ MATTHEW **11:28–30**
Come to me, all you who are weary and burdened, and I will give you rest. Take my yoke upon you and learn from me, for I am gentle and humble in heart, and you will find rest for your souls. For my yoke is easy and my burden is light.

■ JOHN **1:12–13**
Yet to all who received him, to those who believed in his name, he gave the right to become children of God—children born not of natural descent, nor of human decision or a husband's will, but born of God.

■ JOHN **14:6**
Jesus answered, "I am the way and the truth and the life. No one comes to the Father except through me."

■ ACTS **17:24–25**
The God who made the world and everything in it is the Lord of heaven and earth and does not live in temples built by hands. And he is not served by human hands, as if he needed anything, because he himself gives all men life and breath and everything else.

■ ROMANS **4:4–5**
Now when a man works, his wages are not credited to him as a gift, but as an obligation. However, to the man who does not work but trusts God who justifies the wicked, his faith is credited as righteousness.

■ ROMANS **8:1–2**
Therefore, there is now no condemnation for those who are in Christ Jesus, because through Christ Jesus the law of the Spirit of life set me free from the law of sin and death.

■ EPHESIANS **2:8–9**
For it is by grace you have been saved, through faith—and this not from yourselves, it is the gift of God—not by works, so that no one can boast.

■ HEBREWS **10:17–18**
Then [God] adds: "Their sins and lawless acts I will remember no more." And where these have been forgiven, there is no longer any sacrifice for sin.

■ HEBREWS **12:2**
Let us fix our eyes on Jesus, the author and perfecter of our faith, who for the joy set before him endured the cross, scorning its shame, and sat down at the right hand of the throne of God.

NOW, TURN TO PAGE 52

Free.*

Consider any scriptures you circled, then pick the one that seemed to speak to you the most, whether that felt like love, forgiveness, relief or encouragement.

WRITE OUT THE FULL VERSE HERE:

NOW MEMORIZE IT.

TEAR OUT THAT PAGE AND TAPE IT TO A PLACE YOU'LL SEE EVERY DAY.

This is the truth God intends for you.
Committing it to memory (and even repeating it to yourself)
can help you crowd out the other voices—the lies—
that disagree with this truth.

Free.*

Imagine for a moment that the false belief you've held—or a behavior that has stemmed from it—was completely gone, wiped away from your mind and life.

Consider the scripture verse you're memorizing. Imagine what would be different about your life if you really believed and fully received this truth from God.

Write down one thing that you'd imagine or hope would be different in each of the following areas of your life:

WHAT WOULD BE DIFFERENT?

…at home, work or school?

…in my friendships?

HOW DOES CONSIDERING THESE POSSIBILITIES MAKE YOU FEEL?

■ ■ ■ ■

...in my relationship with my spouse (or future spouse)?

...with my family?

...about how I view myself?

...about my relationship with (or thoughts about) God?

Free.*

If you looked up a list of all-time, least-favorite words, "repentance" would probably be near the top of the list.

Unfortunately, repentance has gotten a bad rap. It's not about feeling ashamed and mustering up a strong sense of guilt, it's about making the choice to agree with what God says. It's about turning away from beliefs or behaviors that don't line up with truth, and moving in another direction.

With that in mind, consider the ways any false beliefs you've held about yourself or God have held you hostage.

(If you're at a loss, flip back to pages 24-25 for some practical ways one false belief has infiltrated your life.)

Then, get specific about an action plan for the coming week. Identify at least one belief you want to replace with God's truth—maybe the scripture verse you memorized—and at least one behavior (even if it's small) that you'll choose to replace with a new action.

You'll be asked to record how it's going on a daily basis in the next section.

*
STORY
SCOTT

Being in a place of dependency on God has been freeing for me.
full story on page 106

DORA

I had to create new patterns in my life, and recognize why I was doing things. If it was out of a need to perform for approval, I stopped doing it.
full story on page 103

LIST OF ALL-TIME,
LEAST-FAVORITE WORDS

DIARRHEA	BRIC-A-BRAC
REPENTANCE	SMEAR
GOITER	MOIST
LOAMY	PLUG
KITSCHY	LARD
AKIMBO	PILAF

ACTION PLAN

I CHOOSE NOT TO BELIEVE:

For example: I choose not to believe that my worth comes from what other people think about me.

INSTEAD, I CHOOSE TO AGREE WITH GOD AND BELIEVE:

For example: I choose to believe that God accepts me unconditionally.

I'M GOING TO STOP DOING THIS:

For example: I'm going to stop staying late at the office to impress my coworkers.

INSTEAD, I'M GOING TO DO THIS:

For example: I'll leave the office when my work for the day is finished.

Free.*

Maybe you're starting to see how getting free will change your life. You might even be experiencing a bit of a "lift" or an emotional high. That's a good thing. But it's important not to confuse freedom with "feeling good." Often the things that are best for us in the long run don't feel good in the moment.

Take exercise, for example. Working out gives us freedom of movement and keeps us in shape, but unless we push ourselves beyond our comfort zones, it's useless. In the same way, adopting new beliefs and behaviors—repenting and returning to what God intends for us—might feel uncomfortable after the initial "buzz" passes. That's when quitting becomes a huge temptation.

This is why we need to put our faith in what is true, not in how we feel. Emotions can be deceptive, and we have a vested interest in keeping things as comfortable as possible.

But comfort isn't the goal. It's freedom.

THE PURSUIT OF REAL FREEDOM REQUIRES PERSISTENCE AND ENDURANCE, ESPECIALLY WHEN THINGS GET UNCOMFORTABLE.

FOUR

Some of us love Action Plans—we're check-the-box junkies. Some of us see a to-do list and freak out. And a few of us right now are considering going back just to *tweak* our Action Plans. Don't.

Remember: this is not a self-help process, you're not being graded, and the freedom you can and will experience will definitely change your life. But it is time to move.

IT'S TIME TO THROW YOUR WEIGHT BEHIND THIS PLAN—BECAUSE WHETHER IT TAKES A FEW DAYS OR A DECADE, SOMETHING INCREDIBLE IS WAITING FOR YOU.

Need a reminder of what that might be? Read your own words. (See pages 54–55.)

And here's a plan to get you through your Plan:

Take it one day at a time.

Literally, take this guide out at the end of each day this week to record how things are going.

■ ■ ■ ■

END OF DAY 1

Flip back to your Action Plan on page 57 and write down your
new belief:

INSTEAD, I CHOOSE TO AGREE WITH GOD AND BELIEVE:

Write whatever you committed to do here:

INSTEAD, I'M GOING TO DO THIS:

Now think through your day (what you did this morning, people you talked
to, places you went) then consider what helped you and what held you back
as you worked on incorporating your new belief and action:

THIS HELPED
(or, today's mini-victories)

THIS HELD ME BACK
(or, today's minor setbacks)

WHAT'S GOING THROUGH YOUR HEAD RIGHT NOW?

Maybe it's a conversation you want to have with God,
maybe it's an idea or question you can't shake, maybe it's just
something you don't want to forget. **Record it here:**

DAVID

STORY Reading the Bible and opening up to friends really helped me.
full story on page 105

PRAY

Take a moment to ask God to help you keep your thoughts
focused on his truth about you. Ask Him to fill your mind with
dreams about the incredible freedom he intends for you.*

PHILIPPIANS *4:8 FINALLY, BROTHERS AND SISTERS,
WHATEVER IS TRUE, WHATEVER IS NOBLE,
WHATEVER IS RIGHT, WHATEVER IS PURE,
WHATEVER IS LOVELY, WHATEVER IS ADMIRABLE—
IF ANYTHING IS EXCELLENT OR PRAISEWORTHY—
THINK ABOUT SUCH THINGS.

Free.*

END OF DAY 2

Getting free is a day-by-day thing. The more you're aware of what helps and what holds you back, the easier it gets. It becomes muscle memory—a little less off-roading, a little more Autobahn.

Flip back to your Action Plan and write your new belief here:

INSTEAD, I CHOOSE TO AGREE WITH GOD AND BELIEVE:

Write whatever you committed to do here:

INSTEAD, I'M GOING TO DO THIS:

Think through your day then consider:

THIS HELPED
(or, today's mini-victories)

THIS HELD ME BACK
(or, today's minor setbacks)

WHAT ARE YOU THINKING RIGHT NOW?

★BRETT STORY My biggest test was throwing away a lot of the school stuff in my basement. full story on page 107

PRAY Take a moment to ask God to give you strength to continue to endure as you incorporate these new disciplines of thought and action.*

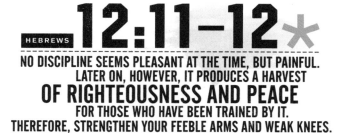

HEBREWS 12:11–12★

NO DISCIPLINE SEEMS PLEASANT AT THE TIME, BUT PAINFUL.
LATER ON, HOWEVER, IT PRODUCES A HARVEST
OF RIGHTEOUSNESS AND PEACE
FOR THOSE WHO HAVE BEEN TRAINED BY IT.
THEREFORE, STRENGTHEN YOUR FEEBLE ARMS AND WEAK KNEES.

Free.*

■ ■■■ DAY 3

END OF DAY 3

Know this by heart? Try it:

What I'm believing:

INSTEAD, I CHOOSE TO AGREE WITH GOD AND BELIEVE:

Write whatever you committed to do here:

INSTEAD, I'M GOING TO DO THIS:

How did it go today?

THIS HELPED
(or, today's mini-victories)

THIS HELD ME BACK
(or, today's minor setbacks)

WHAT ARE YOU THINKING RIGHT NOW?

I rested for the first time in my life, and it was more fun than I can describe! full story on page 102

*STORY
KRISSY

PRAY

Ask God to focus your mind and heart on truth, and the real freedom he intends for you to enjoy. Ask Him to show you where you might be pursuing false freedoms that lead to imprisonment.*

1 CORINTHIANS ***9:24-25**

DO YOU NOT KNOW THAT IN A RACE ALL THE RUNNERS RUN,
BUT ONLY ONE GETS THE PRIZE?
RUN IN SUCH A WAY AS TO GET THE PRIZE.
EVERYONE WHO COMPETES IN THE GAMES GOES INTO STRICT TRAINING.
THEY DO IT TO GET A CROWN THAT WILL NOT LAST; BUT WE DO IT TO GET
A CROWN THAT WILL LAST FOREVER.

Free.*

Orange you glad we didn't say banana?

OK, three days down. If you look back through, you'll probably notice some patterns—things that get in the way of your freedom because they result in unhealthy behavior. It might have to do with environments, relationships, media or even times of day.

God wants us to experience pleasure and joy. This freedom process isn't about "sin management" or putting a bunch of rules around our life. It's about emptying out the unhealthy so there's room to get filled with God's goodness.

LIST ANY PATTERNS YOU'RE NOTICING THAT LEAD TO UNHEALTHY CHOICES.

WHAT'S ONE PRACTICAL THING YOU COULD DO TO REPLACE THAT? *(You might consider the things that helped this week.)*

■ ■ ▓ ▓

FOR EXAMPLE

I feel bad everytime I watch the late local news. ✱ **I'm going to turn off the TV before it comes on and crack a book or go to bed.**

I need friends who encourage one another. ✱ **I'm going to start the trend.**

I'm preoccupied at work with fearful thoughts. ✱ **I'll try to memorize scriptures like 1 John 4:18 ("perfect love drives out fear").**

My drawer is filled with stuff that reminds me of a bad relationship. ✱ **It's time to get rid of it.**

I get way too competitive at the gym. ✱ **I'll get off the treadmill whenever I notice myself competing.**

Reading celebrity magazines makes me depressed about my body. ✱ **It's time for a new subscription.**

The demands of my job are ruining my marriage. ✱ **I'm going to restructure my work, even if it means a pay cut.**

I've got secrets that make me feel guilty. ✱ **I'm going to share these things with people I trust.**

I've sought out people to serve as mentors to me.
full story on page 101

COURTNEY

Free.*

69

Remember: getting free isn't about jumping through the right hoops or correcting your thinking. Freedom comes from a changed heart and a fundamental belief that God is good and intends good things for you, even when circumstances don't seem to line up with that belief.

But sometimes changing your behavior—especially when you've been prone to self-defeating actions—can help you line up your life with truth instead of living out your own version of it.

True freedom is choosing God instead of defaulting to normal selfish or destructive patterns.

True freedom is about receiving what was always yours to claim.

AND THEN,
IT'S ABOUT FEELING THE FREEDOM
TO GIVE IT AWAY.

FIVE

Breaking free requires courage. We have to stare down the things that have kept us imprisoned for years, decide to kick them to the curb, and endure. And it's almost impossible to do this on our own. We need others to encourage us—to **put courage into** us.

In the same way, being truly free means doing this for others, as well. The Bible says it's *for* freedom that Christ has set us free.*

GOD HAS FREED US, IN PART, SO WE CAN PUT COURAGE INTO OTHERS. AS WE DO, WE FIND THAT WE EXPERIENCE MORE FREEDOM, OURSELVES.

GALATIANS
5*1

So let's focus now on being freedom fighters for the people in our life.

- -

Don't worry, it's not as intimidating as it may sound. Just get ready to put some courage into your friends and loved ones—and maybe get a little more freed up in the process.

CREATE A QUICK LIST OF PEOPLE YOU KNOW WELL.

LIST MIGHT INCLUDE:
IMMEDIATE FAMILY, NEIGHBORS, COWORKERS, CLOSE FRIENDS

Don't think about this too hard. Just write down the names that come to mind.

Looking back at your list of people in your day-to-day life, ask God to make three of those names stand out to you as the people you will put courage into this week. (And stay open to the possibility that they're not all going to be from the "people I love to love" camp.)

SPEND SOME TIME TALKING TO GOD ABOUT WAYS— BIG, MEDIUM, SMALL—THAT YOU COULD ENCOURAGE THESE THREE.

Remember, everyone has stuff they're struggling with or that's holding them back from experiencing freedom. Don't point those things out to them (go easy, tiger), but ask God how you could encourage each person in a way that would counteract that hang-up—even in a small way. Write those names and plans on the next page.

CHEAT SHEET FOR HANG-UPS AND COURAGE-BUILDERS

Remember, this is NOT about judging people or breaking the "Hey, I know what's wrong with you!" news. It's about knowing how to offer some specific encouragement that can bring freedom.

Bitterness and anger might look like:
Unwilling to forgive, depression, strong anger towards one person or group, isolation, committed to revenge, violence, focus on how they've been wronged

Encouragement might sound like:
"Whatever's in your past doesn't define who you are today. I think you're an amazing person and you have so much to give others."

NOT:
"The glow from the flag you're burning really brings out the blue in your eyes."

Feeling rejected or unloved might look like:
Desperate for approval, self-centered, clingy, needy, performance-driven, expecting to be hurt or let down, withdrawn, unemotional

Encouragement might sound like:
"I really value your opinion. Please know that I'm always very interested in hearing what you have to say."

NOT:
"You'll always be #6 in my heart (and #6 is pretty high)."

Fear might look like:
Anxiety and stress, focused on what-ifs, imagining hopeless situations and disasters, overly independent, unwilling to open up, controlling

Encouragement might sound like:
"Know that you're loved, no matter what. If there's ever anything you need, I've got your back."

NOT:
"Man up, pansy!"

Religion might look like:
Self-righteousness, insecurity, proud of doing things "right," focused on others' mistakes, gives and receives with "strings attached," unwilling to open up

Encouragement might sound like:
"I don't care about what you do or don't do, I'm just thankful to know you and glad you're in my life."

NOT:
"I love the font you used on your 'Burn In Hell' sign."

1

NAME

WHEN I MIGHT SEE THEM OR A GOOD TIME TO CALL/EMAIL

THE WAY I'LL ENCOURAGE

2

NAME

WHEN I MIGHT SEE THEM OR A GOOD TIME TO CALL/EMAIL

THE WAY I'LL ENCOURAGE

3

NAME

WHEN I MIGHT SEE THEM OR A GOOD TIME TO CALL/EMAIL

THE WAY I'LL ENCOURAGE

10:24-25*
HEBREWS

LET US CONSIDER HOW WE MAY SPUR ONE ANOTHER ON TOWARD LOVE AND GOOD DEEDS. LET US NOT GIVE UP MEETING TOGETHER, AS SOME ARE IN THE HABIT OF DOING, BUT LET US ENCOURAGE ONE ANOTHER.

Free.*

HOW DID IT GO? *Yes, this means you actually have to follow through with it.*

PERSON 1

1 — 2 — 3 — 4 — 5 — 6 — 7 — 8 — 9 — 10

THREW HOT COFFEE IN MY FACE   NAMING A KID AFTER ME

NAME:

Easier than imagined? Unusual response? Follow-up ideas?

PERSON 2

1 — 2 — 3 — 4 — 5 — 6 — 7 — 8 — 9 — 10

GAVE ME A WEDGIE   BUYING A TIMESHARE TOGETHER

NAME:

Easier than imagined? Unusual response? Follow-up ideas?

PERSON 3

```
1       2       3       4       5       6       7       8       9       10
o-------o-------o-------o-------o-------o-------o-------o-------o-------o
└ I THINK I MIGHT HAVE TO MOVE              OFFERED TO HELP ME MOVE ┘
```

NAME:

Easier than imagined? Unusual response? Follow-up ideas?

If you didn't get a good response—or even any response—don't think you failed. Sometimes encouragement takes years to sink in or make sense. Sometimes it's met with skepticism. And sometimes it takes a lot of repetition.

But keep Hebrews 10:24-ing people.

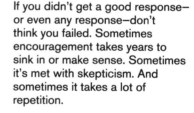

FREEDOM WILL COME. FOR THEM, AND FOR YOU.

★ STORY

MICHAEL

Encouragement from other guys helped me get free.

full story on page 104

Free.*

79

★10:8
MATTHEW

"FREELY YOU RECEIVED, FREELY GIVE."

–JESUS

In God's economy, there's no such thing as scarcity. In fact, the Bible often tells us that one of the ways we receive is by giving.

When we take our eyes off ourselves and instead focus on others, something is unlocked in the spiritual realm.

Hopefully you experienced some of this as you encouraged other people, but it doesn't have to end there. Instilling a discipline of encouragement extends far beyond making a list and checking it twice.

IT MEANS LOOKING FOR "GOD SIGNS" IN OTHER PEOPLE, CALLING THEM OUT AND INSTILLING COURAGE AS A WAY OF LIFE.

STEPPING OUT BOLDLY
TO ENCOURAGE OTHERS
SENDS A POWERFUL
MESSAGE TO BITTERNESS,
FEAR, AND INSECURITY
THAT YOU'RE GOING A
DIFFERENT DIRECTION.

MAKE YOUR DECLARATION.

SIX

God loves a good party.

In the Bible, God told the people of Israel to set aside time and portions of their offerings and commit to throwing a big party. These parties were often celebrations of things God had done in the past, and ways he delivered his people into freedom. It's time to do the same.

Maybe this journey you've been on hasn't seemed as dramatic as God leading a nation of people through a parted sea on dry land, but your journey to freedom is no less revolutionary. Your story is a part of the same freedom story God is telling. Simply choosing to engage is the most difficult part of any journey, and you're already on your way.

It's time celebrate what God is doing and look ahead to the goodness that awaits.

*15:24
LUKE

"FOR THIS SON OF MINE WAS DEAD AND IS ALIVE AGAIN;
HE WAS LOST AND IS FOUND."
SO THEY BEGAN TO CELEBRATE.

WHAT ARE YOU THANKFUL FOR RIGHT NOW?

Don't think too hard about this. Just write down whatever comes to mind.
(And yes, you should definitely include things like football Sundays, your family vacation at the lake and that friend who stuck with you.)

...AND, WHAT ARE YOU LOOKING FORWARD TO?

Big or small, write at least five of those things down.

1

2

3

4

5

6

7

8

Free.*

Spending time reflecting on what we're thankful for and our dreams for the future reveals something deeper: **the joy and hope that come from experiencing freedom.**

As you wrote down what you're grateful for, most likely you experienced feelings of joy. Joy is different from—and often deeper than—happiness. Joy is being content in the moment and engaged with what's in front of you—regardless of what else isn't going well—because you know who God says you are and you believe in his plans for you.*

JEREMIAH *29:11

"FOR I KNOW THE PLANS I HAVE FOR YOU,"
DECLARES THE LORD,
"PLANS TO PROSPER YOU
AND NOT TO HARM YOU, PLANS TO GIVE YOU
HOPE AND A FUTURE."

Hope is the sense that there's something over the horizon—something better—to which God is calling you. Hope gives you the freedom to dream and pursue those dreams. It means believing that God has good things in store for you, even if you don't yet know what those are.*

10:10 * JOHN

I HAVE COME THAT THEY MAY HAVE LIFE.
AND HAVE IT TO THE FULL.

FLIP BACK AND REREAD WHAT YOU WROTE ON PAGES 10-11 ABOUT THE DREAM YOU'RE NOT PURSUING, AND THE REASONS THAT HAVE HELD YOU BACK.

The point of this journey toward freedom you've been on is NOT to get you to pursue that one dream, necessarily. But as you look back on it, do you recognize anything that's held you back that's rooted in a stronghold of some kind? What's different now?

God intends good things for you, and he's given you the ability to dream.

Ask God to give you dreams borne out of freedom, and the courage to pursue them.

WRITE DOWN OR SKETCH OUT ANYTHING THAT COMES TO MIND.

Be open to new thoughts that line up with the truth you've read from scripture.

(Questions about prayer? Turn to page 99.)

Free.*

God has given you a place in the freedom story he's telling. You know how your part of the story begins—it's your life up to this point—and if you've chosen to follow Jesus, you can have confidence and hope in the ultimate, breathtaking end:

Then I heard a loud voice in heaven say: "Now have come the salvation and the power and the kingdom of our God, and the authority of his Christ. For the accuser of our brothers, who accuses them before our God day and night, has been hurled down. They overcame him by the blood of the Lamb (Jesus) **and by the word of their testimony** (stories)**; they did not love their lives so much as to shrink from death."** ✳

12:10–11 REVELATION

Sharing our own stories of freedom is important. It sends a powerful message to bitterness, fear, and insecurity (lies from the enemy) that we are choosing a different direction. Our stories become a declaration of our freedom. ✳ - - - - - - - - - - - - -

ANSWER EACH QUESTION
IN NO MORE THAN ONE OR TWO SENTENCES.

Being succinct and precise can make your story more impactful when you share it.

You might still be working through the process of getting free. That's OK. Sharing your story while you're still working through it can be just as powerful, for you and for others.

ALWAYS BE PREPARED
TO GIVE AN ANSWER TO EVERYONE WHO ASKS YOU
TO GIVE THE REASON FOR
THE HOPE THAT YOU HAVE.
✳**3:15**
1 PETER

STORY ✳
RACHEL

Telling my story to three other women helped me heal. full story on page 100

What's one former belief or behavior from which God is freeing you?

How has that false belief or behavior made you feel?

What was your turning point? How are you making a break?

What practical steps or new behaviors are helping you heal and get free?

If you're feeling any new freedom in this area of your life, what's that like?

Free.*

Your freedom journey doesn't end here.

Hopefully by now you've identified a false belief or behavior that has held you back, and you've taken steps to believe what God says about you. You're moving forward, and it's an exciting time. But you're almost certainly still wrestling with areas where you're not free. That's OK. And things you thought you'd overcome might someday try to crawl back into your life, tempting you like an old bad habit. When that day comes, don't be fooled. You can stand firm and reject that old lie, knowing that God's power has delivered you.

You might find it helps to repeat the process in this guide, but realize that the point isn't the process—or any process. And the power to find freedom doesn't come from more knowledge of strongholds or implementing the right action plan. Don't fixate on a process. Getting free isn't a self-help cleansing ritual.

RELATIONSHIP WITH JESUS IS THE POINT OF OUR FREEDOM. IT'S HIS POWER THAT DELIVERS US WHEN WE TRUST IN HIM.

So stay in the game. Remember the ultimate score. Know your opponent, but stay focused on Jesus and trust God to do what only he can. ✶

*12:2

HEBREWS

LET US FIX OUR EYES ON JESUS,
THE AUTHOR AND PERFECTER OF OUR FAITH,
WHO FOR THE JOY SET BEFORE HIM ENDURED THE CROSS,
SCORNING ITS SHAME, AND SAT DOWN AT THE RIGHT HAND OF
THE THRONE OF GOD.

1:6*

PHILIPPIANS

HE WHO BEGAN A GOOD WORK IN YOU
WILL CARRY IT ON
TO COMPLETION
UNTIL THE DAY OF CHRIST JESUS.

ONE LAST THING.

TURN THE PAGE

No matter how you choose to move forward with your freedom, it's important that you don't go alone.

We are wired for relationships— relationship with God, relationships with others. So write down one thing you'll commit to doing to keep those relationships going, whether that means a commitment to daily prayer, a commitment to studying a certain part of the Bible, or making intentional choices to spend time with a community of people.

WHAT I'M DOING NEXT:

Well, the *very* last thing.
TURN THE PAGE

Free.

THIS IS FREEDOM. THIS IS FOR YOU.

GENTLENESS
LOVE JOY
HOPE
SELF-CONTROL
ACCEPTANCE FORGIVENESS

FAITHFULNESS PATIENCE
PROVISION
SALVATION PEACE
GRACE PEACE
BELONGING

Free.*

APPENDIX

INTERACTING WITH YOUR GUIDE

Here are a few tips that might help as you're thinking about setting aside time each day to spend with your Free guide. These tips are also helpful if you're wanting to set aside time to spend with God each day after this Free journey is finished.

1. CHOOSE A SPECIFIC TIME OF DAY.

It helps to have time on the calendar, and if you treat it just like you would any other meeting or appointment. If you wait for the time to "be right" then you'll probably never get around to it.

2. CHOOSE A SPECIFIC PLACE.

If there's a good chair or a writing desk in your house, those could work well. You could also choose a private place at work or in a coffee shop, but it's better to find a place that's predictable, quiet, and fairly solitary.

3. HAVE YOUR MATERIALS HANDY.

It's good to have at least a pen and something to write on (there is room for notes at the back of this guide), a Bible, your guide, and anything else that would make you more comfortable. Make sure you have whatever you need before you sit down so that you're not distracted in the middle of your time.

4. BE REASONABLE ABOUT YOUR TIME.

Deciding to spend two hours on this might sound noble, but it's probably unrealistic for most people. Set reasonable expectations around time so that you're consistently meeting them. Fifteen to thirty minutes is probably best for most people, but if you really want to do a deeper dive you could plan for as much as an hour.

PERSPECTIVE ON PRAYER

Prayer means communicating with God. It's that simple. There are no right words, it's more than a holiday shout-out, and you don't have to be "good at it" before you try it. Prayer is about you and God developing an intimate, day-in and day-out relationship. And you can start right now.

When you begin talking to God, getting out the first words can feel like the most awkward part. But jump in and see what follows. ("I don't know what to say, God, but this thing happened at work..."). Prayer doesn't need a perfect beginning or end—God's not your English teacher waiting on a five-paragraph essay. Prayer is more like an ongoing conversation that gets more and more comfortable over time.

Be as honest and open as you can. Remember there's nothing you can say to God that he doesn't already know, and you don't have to "clean up your act" before he will listen to you. He could never love you more than he does right now.

Spend time listening. Tell God you want to be present with him for no reason other than to thank him for belonging to him. Then dwell with Him silently. Receive His love.

As prayer becomes more natural, you'll begin to feel God's presence in the conversation. Don't be discouraged if you don't hear an audible voice. Many people who talk to God don't hear his voice in the traditional sense. God works deep in our hearts. It often feels like a prompting, a push toward an answer, or the comfort that comes when you feel someone is listening, responding, and fully loving you—no matter what you've said or done.

> Prayer doesn't need a perfect beginning or end—God's not your English teacher waiting on a five-paragraph essay.

A FEW TIPS ON RECEIVING FROM GOD:

If you're having a hard time focusing, empty your mind of distractions by writing down whatever is interrupting your thoughts. Don't get frustrated if your to-do list pops back into your head at some point. It's not about how often your mind wanders; it's about how often you come back to listening.

Sometimes it helps to visualize a place in your mind—and then bring Jesus into that place. Imagine Him there with you, listening and talking.

Don't get caught up in the kinds of words you're using. Just talk like you would with anyone else in your life. God knows what you're thinking anyway.

If you're having a difficult time, tell God that you're frustrated and can't seem to connect with him. Maybe there's something else that He wants you to focus on.

RACHEL'S STORY ✴

FREEDOM FROM BITTERNESS/ACCUSATION

What's one former belief or behavior from which God has freed you?

I believed that at any moment God might harshly correct me—that he delighted in "teaching me a lesson." I spent so much time thinking about not getting in trouble that I didn't have a personality of my own.

How did that belief or behavior make you feel at the time?

I felt paralyzed to make a move. I over-thought every decision I made at work and in my marriage and friendships to the point of exhaustion. I was anxious about the next time I would sin. Each time I did sin, I braced myself, imagining the worst possible outcome, and beat myself up over my wrongdoing. At any given moment, I had a speech ready in my head about what a terrible person I was, and all the ways I had completely blown it.

IN MY ANGUISH I CRIED TO THE LORD, AND HE ANSWERED BY SETTING ME FREE.
✴118:5 PSALM

What was the turning point? What made you realize you needed to make a break?

I heard someone teach that the job of the enemy is to accuse followers of Christ. That seemed interesting, but I didn't think it had anything to do with me. On the way home from that teaching, I asked God in a prayer, "Does the enemy accuse me?" By the time I got home I was sobbing. It was like a veil lifted, and I could see how trapped I felt in all aspects of my life.

What practical steps, systems, or new behaviors helped you heal and get free?

I told my story to three other women. They loved me by telling me all the ways that God loves me, they shared the value of Jesus dying on the cross so I can't be condemned, and they prayed for me. I asked the Holy Spirit to fill me up in the places that had been full of accusation, and I memorized scripture to defend myself the next time it came knocking.

What does living in freedom in this area of your life look like now?

I have space in my mind now where I used to replay all the ways I'd sinned and those speeches about what a loser I am. Now I interact with the Holy Spirit in that space. I ask for the Lord's correction, and I know that it won't be harsh. I recognize times when I feel accused, and tell the enemy to get lost. Frequently, I remind myself of Psalm 118:5. I know who I am, and how the Lord sees me. I know that He delights in me, and has no plans to squash me to teach me a lesson.

* COURTNEY'S STORY

What's one former belief or behavior from which God has freed you?
I believed that because I didn't grow up in the church and know basic things, God was not as pleased with me as he was with his other children. I felt like God loved me out of obligation and would tolerate me, but that I'd still be an outcast in his kingdom.

How did that belief or behavior make you feel at the time?
I felt suffocated by accusation. In my mind, I would never be good enough, and a constant recording in my head reminded me of this. I felt like no one would accept me for my true self, so I began to morph into what I thought people wanted me to be. My life's purpose became pleasing others, hoping that their acceptance would bring fulfillment and validate my worth.

What was the turning point? What made you realize you needed to make a break?
I attempted suicide when I was in 8th grade. I remember my parents rushing in to save me, and in that moment I felt so loved and protected. So I was confused about why those thoughts resurfaced throughout high school, college and into my adult life. When I began to understand that the negative, nagging thoughts in my mind weren't actually coming from me, I was shocked. I was angry that I had been a pawn in such a sick and twisted game for so long. I was done.

What practical steps, systems, or new behaviors helped you heal and get free?
I now have people in my life who serve as mentors to me. I receive prayer and seek out scripture that provides me with written confirmation of God's truth. I'm also very intentional about what I allow to enter my spirit, whether it's a song, a magazine, a particular environment, criticism, or even praise. If it's anything that would lead me down the path of performance, comparison, or questioning of my self worth, I don't go near it.

What does living in freedom in this area of your life look like now?
I feel free in being more concerned with what God feels for me than what others think of me, and what I've oftentimes thought of myself. There's a peace I feel when I choose to believe God's truth over the enemy's masked lies. Giving my mind over to God is what gives me true freedom, and that feels good!

5:10 * 1 PETER
AND THE GOD OF ALL GRACE,
WHO CALLED YOU TO HIS ETERNAL GLORY IN CHRIST,
AFTER YOU HAVE SUFFERED A LITTLE WHILE,
WILL HIMSELF RESTORE YOU
AND MAKE YOU STRONG, FIRM AND STEADFAST.

For you created my inmost being; you knit me together in my mother's womb. I praise you because I am fearfully and wonderfully made; your works are wonderful, I know that full well.

PSALM **139:13–14**

KRISSY'S STORY

FREEDOM FROM REJECTION

What's one former belief or behavior from which God has freed you?

I believed my identity and worth were tied to what I accomplished. It was a performance addiction that manifested itself in every aspect of my life. One area of bondage was my career: I felt that all my past accomplishments has landed me this "important" job, and I'd do whatever it took to be successful at it. I worked non-stop. I was desperate to be successful because it made me feel important and worthy.

How did that belief or behavior make you feel at the time?

It was a roller coaster. When things were good, I was prideful—I believed my job was really important and I was hot stuff. When things were bad, I was devastated—I felt stupid and incompetent. There was a voice in my head that never shut off, constantly replaying events and telling me that I was amazing or terrible. It was exhausting.

What was the turning point? What made you realize you needed to make a break?

I wasn't looking for freedom when I found it. A friend suggested I pray and ask God to free me from whatever was separating me from Him. At the time, I had no idea what that was, but I felt like there was something. So, I did it—I asked God to break me from whatever was separating me from him. The answer was performance, and a specific manifestation was my job.

What practical steps, systems, or new behaviors helped you heal and get free?

Over the course of a year, I felt like God was telling me to quit my job and do nothing. It seemed like the most absurd thing I'd ever heard. I asked people in my life what they thought of the idea, and they said it was probably the only thing that would keep me from losing my marriage, since I was willing to sacrifice anything for the sake of my career. So I did it—I quit my high-paying, "important" job. It was the most freeing thing I'd ever done. I took a year sabbatical, where my only job was to love God and my husband. It was the first time in my life I'd ever rested, and it was more fun than I can describe!

What does living in freedom in this area of your life look like now?

People who know me well say that when I quit, I looked different physically, even softer. The hard shell of performance had fallen off me. Another miracle is, although I had been diagnosed with fertility issues, just one month after I quit my job I became pregnant without any type of treatment. Now when I look at my daughter, I see freedom in her. Today I battle the need to perform as a mom, but since I know God has delivered me, I catch myself more quickly. My worth is not in my job or even my role as a wife or mom. I know what I'm worth when I reflect on what God says about me, and the price that was paid for my freedom.

What's one former belief or behavior from which God has freed you?
I grew up feeling like I didn't belong—that I was unimportant and not needed. I constantly felt rejected by everyone.

How did that belief or behavior make you feel at the time?
I felt like I needed to "perform" for attention and acceptance. I would hide my true feelings and act like I wasn't hurt or upset when I was. I'd run away from people and relationships when what I really wanted more than anything was for them to run after me. I pushed myself in my career and even hobbies to impress others and earn their approval.

What was the turning point? What made you realize you needed to make a break?
My turning point was a process. First, God started working in my life through relationships with people. My husband saw through my outer shell and challenged my "hard" personality. He wasn't impressed by the achievements I felt made me acceptable to others. That frustrated and challenged me, and I started growing out of habits I'd formed over the years. Second, I went through a Bible study that helped me uncover the reason I did all these things—at my core, I felt rejected. I saw a pattern at work: I believed I was rejected, put up an outer shell to protect myself, and performed to feel accepted.

DORA'S
* STORY

What practical steps, systems, or new behaviors helped you heal and get free?
The antidote to rejection is receiving, and believing and receiving my true identity in Christ has helped me get free. I had to break the agreements I'd made in my heart about being rejected, and stop using the false personality I'd created as a means of feeling acceptance. I had to create new patterns in my day-to-day life, and make conscious choices to recognize why I was doing something. If it was out of a need to perform for approval, I stopped doing it.

What does living in freedom in this area of your life look like now?
Learning to be vulnerable has been an important part of my growth. It feels like I'm finally breathing and at rest. I'm free to be and discover who I am. A career change was a big part of my journey because I realized that the "real" me didn't even like the kind of work I was doing before.

*34:4
PSALM
I SOUGHT THE LORD, AND HE ANSWERED ME;
HE DELIVERED ME FROM
ALL MY FEARS.

*MICHAEL'S STORY FREEDOM FROM FEAR

What's one former belief or behavior from which God has freed you?

My parents separated when I was in 6th grade. It really rocked my world when my dad left. I believed he was walking out on me, too—that I could have been better. After that, I was constantly afraid that any mistake I made would cause a split. This fear lingered and impacted my decisions, actions, and words in just about all facets of my life, personal relationships, work, and even my relationship with God.

How did that belief or behavior make you feel at the time?

I was always anxious—fearful of messing stuff up. This kept me from stepping up in school and work. Once I was willing to take an F in speech class rather than make my speech. I was timid in many areas of my life, just hoping not to rock the boat. I relied on things like alcohol for courage and comfort to help me step out.

What was the turning point? What made you realize you needed to make a break?

The turning point came through interactions with my wife. Often I'd find myself doing things out of fear rather than love. I didn't receive correction well, and took any disagreement as the beginning of the end. I was living in tension, walking on eggshells. I believe the Holy Spirit pointed this out to me—that I was letting fear dictate my life rather than love. This can still rear its ugly head, but I'm able to recognize it more easily now.

What practical steps, systems, or new behaviors helped you heal and get free?

Repenting of agreeing with fear was the biggest step I could take, and I do so continually as I feel it trying to creep back into my life. I also began to spend more time reading the Bible, and meeting with men who looked to encourage and build one another up. Along with behavioral changes, the biggest thing that has helped me get free is the way my wife loves me. She affirms me, builds me up, is thankful for little things, and says she loves me often, usually for no apparent reason. In turn, I feel loved and fear melts away.

What does living in freedom in this area of your life look like now?

It's a very peaceful life. While it's not always easy to execute, it's not complicated. I can look at all of scripture and know it pertains to me. I can read 2 Timothy 1:7 with confidence and know it's true about me. Living in freedom makes life more joyful and relationships less testy. Most importantly, it helps me do what the Lord calls me to do—to trust in him and his promises for my life. It makes me want to help others experience the same freedom.

*1:7
2 TIMOTHY

FOR GOD HAS NOT GIVEN US A SPIRIT OF FEAR, BUT OF POWER AND OF LOVE ---------- AND OF A SOUND MIND.

"This is the covenant I will make with them after that time," says the Lord. "I will put my laws in their hearts, and I will write them on their minds." Then he adds: "Their sins and lawless acts I will remember no more." And where these have been forgiven, there is no longer any sacrifice for sin.

10:16-18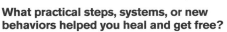

HEBREWS

✳ FREEDOM FROM FEAR

DAVID'S STORY
✳

What's one former belief or behavior from which God has freed you?

I lived for a long time with the idea that God was disappointed with me. I would have called myself a "Christian," but if I were being honest, I thought that at any moment God might revoke that membership card.

How did that belief or behavior make you feel at the time?

I was fearful. I put pressure on myself to "be good." I felt that if I could stack up more good deeds than bad, that would tip the scales for me and I'd sneak my way into heaven, which seemed like the better of two alternatives.

What was the turning point? What made you realize you needed to make a break?

One morning when my three-year-old daughter stumbled in, sleepy-eyed in her pajamas, I realized how much I loved her and how it wasn't because of anything she does, but instead, because of who she is. It hit me that this is how God loves me, only in a more perfect way. I started to realize that it wasn't about heaven and hell—it was about falling into a loving relationship.

What practical steps, systems, or new behaviors helped you heal and get free?

Going back to the Bible and reading it through the lens of God's grace was amazingly freeing. Books of the Bible like Hebrews were like cold water in the desert. It says right there in black and white that there are no longer any sacrifices for sin—they've all been taken care of. Good news, indeed. Sitting under teachers who teach grace, opening up to friends in a small group, and repenting of some fearful beliefs have also been great.

What does living in freedom in this area of your life look like now?

It feels like freedom. It's not up to me to "do" anything. I can choose to respond in love, and that's always good, but it's God's good in me. If I feel like I stumble, I'm forgiven. I don't have to worry about losing my salvation any more than my three-year-old needs to worry about me kicking her out of the house.

* SCOTT'S STORY

What's one former belief or behavior from which God has freed you?

I used to think there was a great mystery beyond God I could solve that would provide the "enlightenment" needed to move me to some deeper understanding of my life. This led me down the "new age" path of consulting spirit guides, past lives, etc. It stemmed from growing up in church and not experiencing any life in the spirit. This wasn't the church's fault, exclusively, but it provided an impetus for me to put myself at the center of the story that met what I perceived to be my needs at the time.

How did that belief or behavior make you feel at the time?

The thing about New Age thought is that there's always something better to be discovered. So I went from the high of feeling like I'd cracked some spiritual nut to feeling empty and craving something else to stroke my ego and tell me I was on the enlightened path of understanding. It's ingenious in its deception. It keeps you on the hook like a drug.

What was the turning point? What made you realize you needed to make a break?

God put his followers in my life. They didn't talk about scripture or ask me if I was "saved," they just hung around my wife and me and we started to notice something different about them. They seemed to have strength and peace—I had no idea that was what following Jesus looked like. After a couple years of these relationships, the roller coaster ride of my spirituality looked pale and weak by comparison. I wanted out. The more I stepped out, the more life in Christ made sense. I started applying the Bible to my life, and understanding that being a "follower" was a positive thing.

What practical steps, systems, or new behaviors helped you heal and get free?

I put myself under spiritual authority with a mentor. I disciplined myself to sit under teaching in my community. I started reading the Bible with a "this is applicable to me" perspective. I tore at my pride by trying to be more humble and open about my sin. I found that openness was the only way to be healed.

What does living in freedom in this area of your life look like now?

Not being on the treadmill of "spiritualism" put me in a place of stillness where I can listen to God for encouragement, teaching, correction, and anything else he has for me. I'm in a place of dependency on God that's freeing for me. I don't have to figure out how to get "better" or on some other spiritual plane. God has already declared my worth, and now my only desire is for more of him. I'm experiencing the "life to the full" that Jesus talks about.

*1:7
2 TIMOTHY

FOR GOD HAS NOT GIVEN US A SPIRIT OF FEAR,
BUT OF POWER AND OF LOVE
---------- **AND OF A SOUND MIND.**

What's one former belief or behavior from which God has freed you?

For many years I had an unhealthy relationship with my school. Some would call it loyalty or school spirit, but it was much deeper than I knew. It led to a shrine of sorts in my basement and allegiances I didn't even know I had. My relationship with my wife and daughter suffered because of my behavior.

How did that belief or behavior make you feel at the time?

It made me feel good. I put value into anything associated with my school, and I lived in denial of a problem. In my mind, I wasn't worshipping an "idol," I was just living like I always had. The problem was that family and friends identified me with my school—they couldn't separate the two. After hearing about strongholds I knew there was a problem.

What was the turning point? What made you realize you needed to make a break?

Learning about strongholds made me think about my behavior in a new light. When my wife observed that my whole identity was wrapped up in my school, that was tough to hear, but it made me realize there was a problem.

* **BRETT'S STORY**

What practical steps, systems, or new behaviors helped you heal and get free?

The biggest test—and my greatest healing—came when my men's small group came over to my house to help me take down all the school stuff in my basement and throw a lot of it away. They really challenged me, and I'm grateful beyond words. The freedom that action provided in my life is remarkable—even my relationships with my wife and daughter are better as a result.

What does living in freedom in this area of your life look like now?

I see myself in a completely different light, and God is walking me through that. I can root for my school, but leave it at that. I know my only allegiance is to God, my provider. I can walk in freedom and know that God will show me the way.

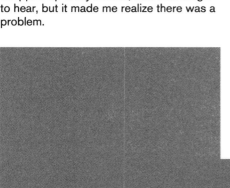

Free
Book*

I am a fanatic about freedom. And I'm fanatical
about coming at you hard in this book. I'm tired
of seeing people beaten down by the world's
systems and by religion. I'm sick of seeing
people live safe, predictable lives while their
God-given passions die. I hate the assumption
that getting close to God means more rules
and restrictions. No more. God's offering real
freedom. Get yours.

Brian Tome

*Nope, sorry. Not that kind of free.

THOMAS NELSON, INC.
Since 1798

"I am a fanatic about freedom. And I'm fanatical about coming at you hard in this book."

Maybe you're not as free as you think you are. Even worse, you may have been duped into believing that a "balanced" life is the key to happiness (it isn't) or that a relationship with God is about layering on rules and restrictions (nope).

Whether it's media-fueled fear, something a parent or teacher said that you just can't shake, or even the reality of dark spiritual forces bent on keeping you down, something is holding you back from the full-on freedom God intends for you.

The Bible says, "Where the Spirit of the Lord is, there is freedom." Not fear. Not guilt. Not morality. *Freedom.* You can have the sort of joy you thought only kids could have. The day of freedom is here.

www.ThomasNelson.com